A Poetic Translation of Chinese Mythology

All rights reserved. No part of this publication may be reproduced, distributed, or transmitted in any form by any means, including photocopying, recording, or other electronic methods without the prior written permission of the author, except in the case of brief quotations embodied in reviews and certain other noncommercial uses permitted by copyright law. For permission requests, write to the author at the email address below.

williamykzhang5@gmail.com

Copyright © 2023 William Zhang
Printed in the United States of America

ISBN: 979-8-218-27297-5

Cover Art & Design by Tell Tell Poetry
Edited by Tell Tell Poetry

First Printing, 2023

To Dominic, Mom, and Dad.

To Alice.

To Micayla, Smaya, Sam, Dylan, Cyrus, Cassia, Ethan, Elizabeth, Jonathan, Erika, Hanjing, Ryogo, Seison, Irmak, Heartlyn, and all my other friends I've made along the way.

TABLE OF CONTENTS

Notes from the Author	ix
Celestial Tapestry	3
Pangu's Sacrifice	7
Nuwa the Creator	9
Shennong's Wisdom	12
Fall of the Monkey King	14
Kuafu Chases the Sun	17
Jing Wei's Sea	20
Yu's Triumph	22
Eight Immortals Cross the Sea	24
Nezha & the Dragon	27
Hou Yi's Loss	30
Jiang Ziya & the Zhou Rebellion	32
Triumphant Love of the White Snake	34
Magpie Bridge	37
Nuwa Mends the Sky	40

NOTES FROM THE AUTHOR

Chinese mythology is a rich tapestry of folklore, legends, and ancient stories that have been passed down through generations. And just as Greek and Roman mythology were the foundation of Western society, Chinese mythology still carries a profound cultural significance even to this day. These myths often embody important cultural, social, and political themes that have shaped Chinese society throughout history.

The myth of the Monkey King is one of the most famous Chinese legends, telling the story of a mischievous and powerful monkey who rebels against the heavens and challenges the celestial order. The Monkey King's defiance of the celestial hierarchy mirrors a recurring theme in Chinese history—the struggle against oppressive rulers and authoritarianism.

Throughout Chinese history, there have been numerous uprisings and revolutions driven by the desire for freedom, justice, and equality. Yet the Monkey King, the great hero, eventually fails. He is still imprisoned by the Buddha. In fact, he is so powerless in the face of the Buddha that he is quite literally being toyed with, then promptly imprisoned for the next five hundred years, perhaps a warning of rebelling against authority in China.

However, the Monkey King's quest for personal freedom and autonomy also mirrors the Chinese people's aspirations for individual liberties. Chinese society has undergone significant transformations, from imperial rule to communist ideology, and individuals have constantly sought personal autonomy and self-expression. The Monkey King's journey symbolizes the human desire for independence and the rejection of constraints imposed by societal norms and political systems.

Another famous myth in Chinese history is that of a cowherd and weaver girl, also known as "Chinese Valentine's Day," a bittersweet love story that portrays the tension between duty and love and the pursuit of true happiness. The tale reflects the enduring influence of social hierarchy and familial obligations in Chinese society. The love between a cowherd and a celestial weaver violates the strict boundaries of social classes. According to the laws of society, they should not, could not, be together. However, they manage to overcome these restraints, reuniting by way of the magpie bridge once a year. A myth that explores a similar theme is "Triumphant Love of the White Snake," although they have a happier ending, as the lovers are able to build a life together.

Chinese myths are not mere stories; they serve as powerful reflections of the underlying cultural, social, and political dynamics in Chinese society. "Fall of the Monkey King," "Magpie Bridge," and "Jing Wei's Sea" are only some of the myths highlighting themes that resonate with the struggles, aspirations, and values of Chinese people. These enduring myths continue to shape the collective consciousness, providing insights into the complex relationship between Chinese mythology, society, and politics.

A POETIC TRANSLATION
OF CHINESE MYTHOLOGY

CELESTIAL TAPESTRY

The origin of the Chinese Zodiac can be traced back to ancient times when the Jade Emperor sought to establish an earthly code. To determine which animals would be part of the Zodiac, a grand race was organized under the moon's gentle light. The cunning Rat, the steadfast Ox, the fierce Tiger, the gentle Rabbit, the majestic Dragon, the wise Snake, the swift Horse, the artistic Goat, the mischievous Monkey, the confident Rooster, the loyal Dog, and the tender Pig all competed. Each animal's placement in the Zodiac was determined by their performance in the race, and thus, the Chinese Zodiac was born—a cycle of twelve animals, each representing a specific year and embodying distinct qualities and characteristics. This celestial tapestry continues to be celebrated and revered, reflecting a rich cultural legacy.

In ancient times, a tale is told,
Of the Chinese Zodiac, a legend of old.
The Jade Emperor called a grand race,
To select the animals, each with grace.

On a certain day, at the river's edge,
The animals gathered, lined along the ledge.
From far and wide, they came with might,
Twelve in total, ready for flight.

The Rat, clever and quick-witted it seems,
Sought the Ox's strength to fulfill its dreams.
So, in a sly move, it hopped on its back
And rode through the fields, leaving no track.

As the duo crossed the river's flow,
The Rat leaped forward, to claim its show.
With cunning tactics, it won the race,
And became the first, in this glorious chase.

Behind him came the steadfast Ox,
Enduring and patient, no paradox.
As he crossed the line, the crowd roared—
Second place to this beast, kindness in his core.

Then emerged the Tiger, fierce and bold,
With fiery grace, its stories unfold.
Swift and mighty, it roared with pride,
Taking third place in this Zodiac stride.

Next, the Rabbit, gentle and kind,
Hopping with grace, with peace in mind.
The emperor praised its soft nature
And granted it the fourth position, a treasure.

Following closely, the Dragon took flight,
A symbol of power, majestic and bright.
With celestial scales and mythical lore,
The emperor placed it fifth forevermore.

Then the Serpent slithered, elegant and wise,
Coiling and gliding, it mesmerized.
The sixth spot was given to this creature so sly,
For its wisdom and charm caught the emperor's eye.

The Horse, with its strength and swift pace,
Galloped onwards, showcasing its grace.
With a thundering stride, it claimed its domain,
And became the seventh in the Zodiac chain.

Seizing the moment, the Goat appeared,
With a gentle demeanor, so calm and revered.
The emperor recognized its peaceful embrace,
Bestowing upon it the eighth heavenly place.

The Monkey, mischievous and full of glee,
Swung through the trees, agile and free.
With its antics and tricks, it earned a name,
The ninth position, forever to claim.

The radiant Rooster, with its resplendent crow,
Announced its arrival, with confidence to show.
With flamboyance and pride, it took to the stage,
Becoming the Zodiac's tenth page.

Then came the loyal Dog, faithful and true,
Barking with joy at the friendships it drew.
The emperor admired its devotion and might,
Granting it the eleventh spot, shining so bright.

Lastly, the Pig, adorned with charm,
Delighting the crowds with its oink and disarm.
The twelfth position, it warmly embraced,
Completing the Zodiac, with its presence encased.

And so, the tale of the Zodiac was born—
A celestial order, in which animals adorn,
Their characteristics and traits forever entwined,
In the Chinese Zodiac, a legacy enshrined.

PANGU'S SACRIFICE

The story of "Pangu Opens the Sky" is like the first seven days of the Christian Bible—the origin story of the universe. Pangu, a giant formed from an embryo in the chaotic universe, awoke from his slumber and found himself trapped within the egg. Determined to break free, he unleashed his divine power and shattered the cosmic egg into two halves. The lighter elements rose to form the sky, while the denser elements sank to create the Earth. To ensure the elements would remain separate, Pangu held open the newly formed cosmos, and for another 18,000 years, Pangu continued to grow, becoming a colossal figure who held the sky firmly in place. His head reached the clouds, his feet rooted deep within the Earth, and his body expanded to fill the space between. After his tremendous efforts, Pangu eventually realized his time was coming to an end. Feeling his energy wane, he decided to rest and peacefully departed from the world. As he lay down, his body transformed into the natural elements of the Earth—the mountains, the rivers, the trees, and all living creatures.

Nothing. There was nothing.
Only the chaotic energy of Yin and Yang.
In that an embryo forms,
Rising from the churning sea of energy.

After ten thousand years of slumber,
The embryo finally awakens—
Out steps Pangu, wielding the ax of creation.
With one mighty swing, the energy splits,
Yin and Yang rises and sinks.

They want to mold together,
To go back to nothing.
But Pangu steps between them,
Holding up the universe with his bare hands.

Eighteen thousand years pass,
And it is finally time for Pangu's collapse.
His breath turns to wind;
His voice becomes the bellowing thunder;
His eyes become the sun and moon;
His blood becomes the rivers and oceans;
His body turns to the mountains and plains—
He finally rests so the world may begin.

NUWA THE CREATOR

In the story of Nuwa creating humans, the Earth is depicted as desolate and lifeless. Witnessing this plight, Nuwa, a serpentine goddess, takes compassion upon the world. With great care, she molds figures of mud, infusing them with life, thus giving birth to the first human beings. With meticulous artistry, she creates the red string of fate, connecting the souls of humanity, and through her divine touch, she breathes purpose and destiny into each human as they embark on a journey of trials, triumphs, and love. Nuwa's legacy endures, guiding humanity through the tapestry of existence, as her creation carries her essence and the eternal bond of connection.

Desolate and barren,
The Earth devoid of life.
Winds howling in loneliness,
As if crying in strife.

But one destined day,
On a cold desert night,
A serpentine goddess
Finally sees their plight.

From Nuwa's gentle touch,
A symphony of creation unfurls.
Her hands, with delicacy unmatched,
Shape beings from earthly swirls.

In her eyes, a shimmering light shone,
A reflection of love's purest grace.
She breathes life into each form,
Nurturing their souls in her embrace.

As the clay takes on a human guise,
Nuwa tenderly weaves
In every breath and beating heart,
The essence of humanity we all perceive.

With meticulous artistry,
She crafts destinies intertwined—
The red string of fate, a testament
To souls destined to align.

Desolate no more, the Earth awakens,
A canvas of life painted anew.
With Nuwa's grace and boundless love,
Let humanity's story forever continue.

SHENNONG'S WISDOM

Shennong, the legendary emperor and patron of Chinese medicine, embarked on a momentous journey. Armed with an insatiable curiosity and unwavering determination, he ventured into the verdant depths of nature to taste the herbs that held secrets of healing. With each delicate leaf and fragrant blossom, Shennong immersed himself in a sensory symphony, braving the bitterness of gentian root and the aromatic sweetness of honeysuckle. As the Earth embraced his every step, Shennong's wisdom grew, and with it, the profound knowledge that would shape the future of herbal medicine for generations to come. While it's not agreed upon whether Shennong was a real Chinese ruler or merely a mythical figure, his impact on Chinese medicine is undeniable, as he created the first medicine book in Chinese history.

Amidst the land of old where legends dance,
Shennong, emperor-wise, begins a noble quest
To taste the herbs of the world.

With robes adorned, he wanders deep
Through valleys, forests,
Riverbeds, and mountain ranges.

His spirit bold and his senses sharp,
He wishes to taste the essence of each herb unseen.
He plucks the leaves with gentle grace—
From fragrant ginseng to tangy rue,
Dandelion's bitter and licorice's sweet—
Each tells tales of life before the unknown.

Shennong samples the symphony of nature's healing,
Unfolding secrets hidden within Mother Earth.
Shennong knew, in the herbs' embrace,
Lay cures for ailments, a gift from above.

Thus through valleys green, he roams with care,
In search of remedies to all of life's burdens.
And so, the herbs whisper their ancient lore
To Shennong's ears, forevermore.
In the tapestry of time, his legacy rests,
As healer and sage, he forever strives.

FALL OF THE MONKEY KING

In the beginning, the Monkey King was born from a stone egg on the Mountain of Flowers and Fruit. As he grew, he became aware of his extraordinary abilities and desires to establish himself as a powerful and immortal being. Thus, the Monkey King ascended to heaven, demanding the Jade Emperor assign him a position within heaven as a deity. However, the Jade Emperor, aware of the Monkey King's rebellious behavior, dismissed him and assigned him a lowly position as the Keeper of the heavenly Stables. Enraged by this insult, the Monkey King rebelled and created chaos in heaven. The Jade Emperor and the other heavenly deities were unable to subdue the Monkey King due to his incredible abilities. Desperate for a solution, they sought the help of the Buddha, who used his divine powers to make himself appear smaller and weaker than the Monkey King. Confident in his abilities, the Monkey King accepted the challenge and displayed his incredible strength and magical feats. He leapt through the Furnace of Eight Trigrams and traveled to the ends of the universe, believing he had won. However, the Monkey King discovered that he was merely traveling inside of the Buddha's hand. Humiliated, the Monkey King tried to flee, but as the Buddha flipped over his hand, the Monkey King was left imprisoned under the Mountain of Five Fingers. This tale shows the arrogance of the Monkey King as he challenges heaven, but with his fall he learns there are deities more powerful than himself.

Born from a stone on a mountain's crest,
The Monkey King was talented beyond compare.
He sought all the vanities of life—
Recognition, fame, power—he wanted it all.
Thus, he challenged heaven's reign.

With pride as vast as the sky above,
He soared above to the Jade Emperor's Palace
And demanded his place with a haughty gaze.
But the emperor returned a disdainful look,
And sent the Monkey King to menial ways:

The Keeper of Stables, a lowly role,
A mockery of his power and might.
Fiery wrath consumed his heart,
And as he unleashed chaos with fury untamed,
His powers blazed, his rage unchained.

Heavens trembled as he rampaged.
Generals, warriors—they fell to his might
As he vandalized the halls with mischievous glee.
Celestial peaches he plopped in his mouth;
Elixirs of immortality he downed like water.

Desperate, the deities sought aid divine,
Then the Buddha, humble, masked his true form
And challenged the Monkey King to a contest of strength.
Convinced of his own victory, the Monkey King
Leapt to the edge of the universe to prove his might.

He left his mark and laughed with pride,
Backflipping back to face the Buddha.
But as he returned he saw to his horror,
His marking on the Buddha's hand.
With his pride crushed he admits defeat—
Now imprisoned for centuries under a mountain's foot.

KUAFU CHASES THE SUN

"Kuafu Chases the Sun" is about the warrior Kuafu's quest to capture the sun. Many people had long been suffering under the sun's scorching heat; Kuafu, the great warrior he was, vowed to tame the sun so the people would no longer suffer. Thus, he began his journey of chasing after the sun, running after it day by day. However, he eventually tires out, and on his dying breath, he realizes how foolish his dreams were. His tale reflects on ambition, the human desire for greatness, and the ultimate realization of our limitations.

A POETIC TRANSLATION OF CHINESE MYTHOLOGY

In an ancient tale, there was a man,
Kuafu, his name, who embarked to capture the sun.

With boundless stride and unwavering might,
He raced across mountains for days on end.

Through valleys deep and rivers long,
He ran and ran across all the land.

But still the sun stood,
Aloft in the endless sky,

Glowing with all its radiant light,
As if taunting him, mocking him, shaming him.

But Kuafu, determined, would not relent,
Still believing he could seize its golden halo.

Yet the sun, elusive, continued to flee,
Its brilliance forever beyond his reach.

Eventually his steps grew weary, his breath grew thin—
As the sun scorched the earth, his vigor departed.

With each stride, he felt the searing heat,
His pursuit, but a dream he could never hold;

His ambition, but a flame all burnt out.
And at the river's edge, he met his end—

WILLIAM ZHANG

Lost to the depths—
Swallowed by the night.

JING WEI'S SEA

In "Jing Wei Fills the Sea," we are introduced to a young maiden named Jing Wei, born of mortal and heavenly lineage. Filled with compassion, she witnesses the sorrow and suffering caused by the insatiable sea. Determined to bring solace, she embarks on a courageous mission to fill the sea. With her wings of pure white, she descends from the heavens, tirelessly dropping rocks of love and hope into the vast ocean. Through unwavering devotion and resolve, Jing Wei's efforts gradually transform the sea, taming its hunger and bringing forth harmony. Her tale serves as an inspiring reminder of the power of selflessness and the ability to make a positive impact in the face of overwhelming challenges.

Jing Wei, the young maiden with wings of pure white,
Soared through the heavens,
But when she descended upon the Earth,
She witnessed pain and resolved to bring solace.
Her heart brimming with compassion, she beheld the sea—
Endless and mighty, its depths unknown.
But the sea, relentless, swallowed the land,
Its boundless appetite left many sorrowful sighs.

Seeing the suffering and the sorrow,
Jing Wei vowed to fill the sea, transforming its demand.
She fluttered her wings, as hope danced in her eyes;
She flew to a faraway land, bringing pebbles and sticks,
Dropping them in a futile effort.

Days turned to months, and months to years—
Jing Wei's resolve grew stronger, unyielding.
She whispered to the waves, her voice a soothing hymn,
Calling forth harmony, where tumult once was.
And so, the sea did yield, inch by inch—
Its hunger tamed, its depths now serene and free.
Jing Wei, the guardian, fulfilled her sacred endeavor—
A testament to courage, boundless and forever.

YU'S TRIUMPH

"The Great Yu Controls the Water" follows the extraordinary journey of Yu, a humble mortal who becomes a legendary figure in ancient China, and his relentless determination to combat the devastating floods that plague the land. With unwavering perseverance and ingenious engineering skills, Yu establishes a system of dikes, canals, and river channels, ultimately mastering the art of water control. Through his dedication and the divine blessing bestowed upon him, Yu triumphs over the raging waters, safeguarding the people and transforming the perilous flood-prone landscape into a prosperous realm. This enduring legend embodies the timeless themes of human resilience, the pursuit of harmony with nature, and the transformative power of individual courage and leadership.

Floods roared and ravaged wide,
Destroying crops and swallowing land.

But Yu, with his heart ablaze and spirit true,
Vowed to save the crying Earth.

Through mountains high and valleys deep,
He toiled, determined and focused.

He carved canals, with sweat and blood,
Guiding rivers to a peaceful road.

With divine blessing upon his brow,
Yu tamed the waters to protect his people.

He bound the rivers and bridged the lands,
Creating a symphony of currents to serve the people.

From desolation, prosperity grew.

EIGHT IMMORTALS CROSS THE SEA

The story of "The Eight Immortals Crossing the Sea" follows a group of mythical beings who embark on a journey to attend the Feast of the Gods. Throughout the journey, each immortal displays their power and personality, each symbolizing different aspects of life, as they travel across the ocean to where the feast is held, creating the famous image.

WILLIAM ZHANG

In the vast expanse where sea meets sky,
Eight Immortals set forth
to attend the feast of the Gods.

Li Tieguai, the beggar,
with gourd in hand,
healing wounds with love and care.

Han Xiangzi, the scholar,
with melodies of gold—
his flute's sweet notes, a celestial chant.

Zhang Guolao, the priest,
atop a white donkey,
using fish drum's beat to quell fatigue.

Lan Caihe, the dancer,
in garments tattered,
embracing chaos to find grace.

He Xiangu, the maiden,
radiant and pure,
bestowing blessings to those in need.

Cao Guojiu, the general,
with righteousness ablaze,
protecting justice across the lands.

Lu Dongbin, the sage,
wisdom's guiding light,
his sword of truth piercing the darkest night.

Zhongli Quan, the elder,
serene and calm,
embodying harmony and bridging realms of myths.

Together they traverse
across unforgiving sea—
a moral odyssey beneath the azure sky.

NEZHA & THE DRAGON

Nezha finds himself facing a formidable opponent in the form of a dragon who has caused chaos and destruction in the region. Nezha, armed with his divine weapons and unwavering determination, engages in a fierce battle with the dragon. Their clash unleashes a spectacle of elemental forces as Nezha's fiery attacks and lightning-fast movements collide with the dragon's immense strength. Despite the dragon's ferocity, Nezha harnesses his inner power and strategic skills, ultimately outmaneuvering and defeating the mighty creature. Through his victory, Nezha not only safeguards the people from the dragon's rampage but also demonstrates the triumph of bravery and righteousness in the face of adversity.

There was once a village by the sea,
Where its villagers worshiped the Dragon of the East.
Every year they offered a banquet
Of pork and beef, of mutton and veal.
But the dragon became greedy, and thus, it roared,

"Only the young boys and girls
Would ever satisfy my appetite."
But the villagers refused with a look of horror.
So the Dragon of the East unleashed its fury,
Its scales gleaming with wicked glitter.

Village roads engulfed with flames,
Its murderous rampage would never be stopped.
But one boy, Nezha donned his celestial gear—
With wheels of fire beneath his feet,
He soared to the battlefield to challenge the beast.

The heavens trembled, the earth quaked,
As Nezha faced the dragon for humanity.
The elements clashed as the combatants danced;
The sky turned dark and trembled with fright as
Fire and water clashed in the sky.

Thunder and lightning roared as the duo fought—
Blow after blow, neither would budge.
The dragon, with all its fury unleashed,
Bellowed loud enough to shake the heavens,
But Nezha, undaunted, stood his ground.

WILLIAM ZHANG

He danced with grace, as swift as the wind—
A hurricane of flames, evading the assault,
Until finally his spear, a blazing streak of light,
Pierced through the dragon's scaly spine.
And with a final surge of divine might,

Nezha's blow shattered the dragon's heart.
And thus, peace was restored, serenity returned.

HOU YI'S LOSS

Hou Yi saw the plight of humanity when all ten suns rose together, so he used his own archery to shoot nine down, and for that, he was granted immortality. Despite the promises of godhood, Hou Yi willingly gives up that immortality to stay with his wife, Chang'e. All Hou Yi wanted was a quiet life with his wife, but the greed of the men he saved is what dooms him. As his student tries to take the elixir of immortality for himself, Chang'e, in a moment of panic after discovering the student's nefarious plan, drinks the elixir to stop it from falling into the wrong hands, thereby ascending to immortality and forever parting from Hou Yi.

Why am I here,
I, Hou Yi, the greatest archer of all,
Hidden within forests?

When ten suns rose to scorch the earth—
It was I who scaled the highest mountains;
It was I who drew my bow and shot;
It was I who let the arrows fly;
It was I who struck down nine of the suns;
It was I who gave the people their peace.

And when all was said and all was done,
It was I who was given the right to godhood;
It was I who held the elixir to immortality;
It was I who gave it up for my love.

But it was also I who was betrayed.
It was my student, one of the many I saved,
Who tried to take the elixir for himself.
It was my wife, whom I gave up godhood to love
Who was forced to ascend to godhood.
It was me who gave everything—

My archery for the lives of the people,
My godhood for the love of my life.
It was me who ended up with nothing.

JIANG ZIYA & THE ZHOU REBELLION

The Investiture of the Gods, known in China as *Fengshen Yan Yi*, is an epic novel written about the transition from the Shang Dynasty to the Zhou Dynasty. King Zhou of the Shang Dynasty, under the influence of the fox demon, Daji, caused nothing but chaos and suffering during his reign. Witnessing the plight of mankind, the gods of heaven enlist Jiang Ziya, a skilled strategist, among other powerful gods, to lead the Zhou forces in rebellion.

In the Shang Dynasty's waning reign,
King Zhou was consumed by hate and rage.
With the fox demon, Daji, as his guide,
Chaos thrived, leading life astray.
The gods of heaven, moved by the plight of man,
Decided to aid the Zhou Dynasty's fight.

Jiang Ziya, a strategist renowned;
Nezha, a warrior with a holy flame;
Yang Jian, a deity with powers divine—
Together, they raged in battle against evil,
Warriors of heaven to restore peace on Earth.

Loyalties tested, destinies entwined,
As forces clashed, the world order reforged.
Through valleys deep and mountains high,
The investiture unfolds beneath the sky.
A tapestry woven with myth and lore,
An epic tale that forever shall endure.

TRIUMPHANT LOVE OF THE WHITE SNAKE

The story of the White Snake, set in Hangzhou during the Song Dynasty, follows the love between a mortal scholar, Xu Xian, and a thousand-year-old White Snake spirit, Bai Suzhen. When the monk, Fa Hai, exposes Bai Suzhen's true nature to Xu Xian, the couple remains devoted to each other. However, soon after Fa Hai visits, Xu Xian's physical health deteriorates. Fa Hai poisoned him. Bai Suzhen seeks a cure for Xu Xian's illness, saving him with a magical herb. The final battle with Fa Hai ensues, and Bai Suzhen's power as a White Snake triumphs. Xu Xian and Bai Suzhen reunite and live a life filled with love and harmony. Even though they were separated by societal expectations, as demonstrated by Fa Hai, they prevailed and ultimately could be happy together.

In Hangzhou's city fair, a tale was spun—
Xu Xian, a scholar, walked by West Lake's shore,
Where his fate intertwined with Bai Suzhen,
A White Snake spirit who longed for love to share.
Their eyes met; their hearts locked in dance—

Bound by affection, their love took flight;
In marriage, they vowed to cherish their life.
Yet Fa Hai, a monk, cunning and scheming,
Saw through Bai Suzhen's guise, saw the snake underneath.
He warned Xu Xian of the spirit's deceit,

To try and break their bond and banish their love.
But it was relentless; it could not be moved.
Xu Xian, devoted, would not betray his wife,
But Fa Hai, unyielding, devised a plan.
A potion, he offered Xu Xian, imbued and disguised.

After a sip, Xu Xian began to fall ill,
And Bai Suzhen, desperate, knew not what to do.
She scaled Mount Emei to find a cure for her lover,
And at the Golden Mountain Temple, her plea was heard—
With a magical herb bestowed, her spirits lifted.

Herb in her grasp, she returned to his side,
Revealing her truth, her serpentine form.
Yet Xu Xian still loved her, despite her appearance,
And she healed him swiftly; their love prevailed,
But Fa Hai returned, his cunning unmasked.

Accusing her of evil, he aimed to divide,
But Bai Suzhen fought, her power divine.
Transforming into floods, she fought for their fate.
And when all was said and all was done,
The lovers reunited and lived a life so serene.

MAGPIE BRIDGE

The Weaver Girl is an immortal goddess, in charge of weaving the beautiful clouds in the sky. However, when she comes down to Earth to bathe, the Cowherd stumbles upon her and they fall in love. The Weaver Girl abandons her heavenly duties to be with the Cowherd, and the two of them build a happy family together, giving birth to a son and daughter. But the Heavenly Mother soon finds out that the Weaver Girl has gone missing and sends the heavenly troops after her.

Leaving the Cowherd and their children behind on Earth, the Weaver Girl is forced to weave clouds in the heavenly realm once again. The couple can only look at each other from afar, their hearts filled with longing and sorrow.

Moved by their deep love and the family's misery, the magpies decide to help. Once a year, on the seventh day of the seventh lunar month, thousands of magpies form a bridge over the Silver River, allowing the family to reunite for a single day.

I am but a mortal cowherd—
Nothing to my name but a house in the woods.
Yet the day I saw her,
I knew she was my destiny.

Weaver of clouds,
Servant of the Heavenly Mother—
Her beauty unmatched;
Her form superior to all.

But I cared not for where she was from,
And she cared not for who I was.
Mortal, immortal—it never mattered;
We knew we would stand by each other's side.

Together we built a family all would envy—
Two beautiful children, a humble home.
But the wrath of the Heavenly Mother
Still loomed above, a mountainous shadow over our heads.

And one day, it happened—
The heavenly soldiers descended.
They took my Weaver Girl,
Tried to take her back to her heavenly duties.

I begged and I pleaded to no avail—
Heavenly orders must be obeyed.
All I could do was merely look on,
Look on as my love was ripped from my hands.

As if to kill my hopes even more,
To stomp them into the ground one final time,
The Heavenly Mother drew a river of stars
Forever separating our family.

But then, on the seventh day of the seventh month
A flock of magpies came to my aid,
Built a bridge stretching across the sky,
Reuniting me with my lover.

A brief moment stolen from the gods. One day a year.

NUWA MENDS THE SKY

The sky, once whole and unified, was torn apart, causing devastation and despair. In response to this dire situation, Nuwa, a compassionate and wise goddess, embarked on a quest to restore harmony. With determination, she collected fragments of the celestial realm, delicately shaping them into intricate pieces. Employing molten gold, she meticulously fused the fragments together, bridging the chasms that marred the heavens. With each stroke of her divine touch, Nuwa crafted a magnificent tapestry of colors and light, weaving a masterpiece that spanned the vast expanse of the firmament. As her work neared completion, the heavens radiated with resplendent beauty, exuding hope and tranquility. Nuwa's efforts culminated in a restored sky, whole and unblemished, bringing joy and relief to all. Her act of mending the sky symbolizes the power of love, dedication, and artistic prowess, as well as her compassion and resolve, forever inspiring generations to cherish the beauty of the heavens and the transformative potential of perseverance and creativity.

The pillars of the sky, cracked and broken.
The dome of heaven, destroyed and fallen.
Heavens wept and stars grew dim,
Gods and mortals in despair.

The firmament, once whole,
Torn asunder, across the land.
The breach, a wound,
Brought sorrow deep—chaos reigned.

But Nuwa, a goddess, with a heart so wise,
Set her eyes to mend the skies.
With her tender touch and artisan's grace,
Nuwa sought to heal the sacred Earth.

She gathered fragments of azure hue.
With molten gold and liquid fire,
She shaped and molded her heart's desire.
Her hands sculpted with care—

Creating wonders to bridge the divide,
Binding heaven and Earth.
Through dedication, Nuwa restored
The vast expanse of heaven.

No longer fractured, no longer torn—
The sky was reborn.
Nuwa, her task complete—
A celestial gift, mending the sky.

www.ingramcontent.com/pod-product-compliance
Lightning Source LLC
Chambersburg PA
CBHW060221050426
42446CB00013B/3135